Widows At The Club

Book Design & Production:
Columbus Publishing Lab
www.ColumbusPublishingLab.com
LCCN: PENDING

Copyright © 2025 by
Bea Gardner

All rights reserved.
This book, or parts thereof, may not be
reproduced in any form without permission.

Paperback ISBN: 978-1-63337-950-3

Printed in the United States of America
1 3 5 7 9 10 8 6 4 2

Widows At The Club

a two-act play by
Bea Gardner and David Russell

It's funny It's poignant It's nostalgic

To the memory of **David Russell**, my partner and co-writer, who helped bring this story to life. Your guidance and support, and especially your theater background made it all possible.

Foreword

Widows at the Club

The setting for **Widows at the Club** is a round table in a country club where three widowed friends in their 70's have been meeting for cocktails and dinner every Wednesday since they met one another on the golf course some 40 odd years ago.

They talk about life, such as parenting that never ends, coping with technology, and things that were taboo way back when. Our three widows at the club are experimenting with the possibility of online dating.

In this two-act play, you will see that not all our widows are eager to change. Rising to the challenge of one's life after the death of a spouse can become a mixed bag of confusing possibilities.

Today, widows and widowers are increasingly evident in the over-seventy population. They have a plethora of common experiences and stories to tell. They are dealing with the complexities of living at a time when everything is changing faster than any of them would like.

Widows At The Club

Their memories of days past and their frustrations with their new lives in a world that seems intent on rushing by without them surely will touch everyone.

In **Widows at the Club**, Becky, Daisy, and Judith struggle with the concept of meeting a man online. In fact, they struggle with the thought of even wanting a man in their lives.

It's funny   It's poignant   It's nostalgic

Act I - Scene 1

First Week of December at the Club

[Becky takes the center seat and Daisy sits with her back to the entrance. Becky raises her hand and circles her wrist to indicate that their drinks can be delivered.]

DAISY: Our drinks at the flip of your wrist. You know, I think it's amazing how you've trained the wait staff here at the club.

BECKY: I didn't train them. They're just giving us good service after all these years.

DAISY: I was just thinking about that the other day. We've been doing cocktails and dinner 'most every Wednesday for about forty years. That's almost two thousand Wednesdays and yet we've never run out of interesting conversation. And Judith is almost always late. Wow! What a remarkable track record!

BECKY: Tonight, I wish Judith were here on time. I'm so excited to talk to both of you about something.

Widows At The Club

DAISY: What are you talking about?

BECKY: Darn that Judith. You'll have to wait until she gets here.

DAISY: I love it when you get your panties in a knot. Come on, Becky, tell me what you're so excited about.

BECKY: Let's just wait for Judith. So, how was your Thanksgiving?

DAISY: Just like I expected! The grandkids are in their own world... texting, not talking, Heather's husband is glued to a football game and she is busy doing all the work. ... So how was your Thanksgiving?

BECKY: Well, you know Jacob couldn't be there. Rivka hosted the dinner and I met Zack's new girlfriend. She was the highlight of the day. The rest of the weekend I spent organizing stuff. I was throwing out some old health magazines and I found an ad ... <u>a full-page ad</u> ... and there he was, the former presidential candidate, Bob Pineapple. You know, Daisy, I find it hard to believe that a man who ran for president of the United States was advertising for a drug to give him an erection.

DAISY: Yeah, "hard" to believe, Becky.

BECKY: Good one, Daisy. Advertising sure has changed since we were kids!

Act I - Scene 1

DAISY: I can remember when advertisements on TV were done in song like... "You'll wonder where dah dah dah dah, dah dah dah dah dah dah dah dah dah."

[Listen to the "Pepsodent Toothpaste Classic TV Commercial (1948)" on YouTube to get the right tune. Anyone who is over 70 will know if you get it right.]

BECKY: Oh, yeah. The Pepsodent jingle. We should make up a song for a Viagra Ad. Hmmm. Maybe it could go something like this: ... "You'll wonder where the drooping went, when you take blue pills, they're heaven sent." [Beat]

DAISY: Or ... "You'll wonder when he went downhill." [Gesture going downhill with drooping finger.] "Could he need the Viagra pill?" [Beat]

BECKY: Or ... Elizabeth, Elizabeth, wherefore art thou? I took the pill and can do it, now!

DAISY: New career! We should be writing for TV!

BECKY: I don't think TV is ready for us!

[Becky and Daisy are laughing out loud when Judith enters and signals for her drink.]

JUDITH: What are you two laughing about?

BECKY: We were just talking about E.D...

JUDITH: E.D.? Oh, I know two girls who have eating disorders. [Beat]

BECKY: Judith, we weren't talking about eating disorders. We were talking about Erectile Dysfunction.

JUDITH: Ohhh!

DAISY: I heard that men are dancing in the streets over Viagra!

JUDITH: Eew!

BECKY: Oh, Judith!

DAISY: Becky, since we're all here now, what do you want to tell us that had you so excited a few minutes ago?

BECKY: Oh, this is going to be great! Such fun!

DAISY: What's going to be fun?

BECKY: Let's do **online dating!** [Beat]

JUDITH: What?

BECKY: We can do this. We can do this. We can compare notes and share stories! I think it'll be exciting!

Act I - Scene 1

DAISY: What?

BECKY: What? What's the matter? You look like I just killed your favorite pet! Can't you see the possibilities?

DAISY: Fun? You call that fun?

BECKY: It could be a shared experience! We can laugh! We can cry! We can live again!

DAISY: Live again? Mr. Wonderful sure didn't make me feel alive! Why would I want to relive that?

BECKY: Oy, your husband really was a schmuck, wasn't he, Daisy?

DAISY: Yep, once a schmuck always a schmuck. He was a good provider, but a sneak and a cheat. It's no wonder he died of a heart attack while in bed with his <u>mistress</u>. ... And now you want me to meet another man?

JUDITH: Don't forget. You were the one in the Will. She didn't get anything. Only a creepy visit from the police.

BECKY: Maybe you could find a real mensch that will make you happy one day. You certainly deserve it.

DAISY: Oh, yeah, riiight, I need a man in every corner of my bedroom and maybe two in the kitchen for good measure... Uh huh, like a hole in the head....

Widows At The Club

[Prop person delivers drinks. Ladies ad lib thank-you's.]

JUDITH: Becky, you're always so busy at the store. What made you think of online dating?

BECKY: Well, when I met Zack's new girlfriend at Thanksgiving dinner, I asked him how they met. He said they met online. I said, "Online? Like buying a girlfriend on Amazon?" "Gramma," he said, "You meet them by getting on a dating site."

DAISY: What's a dating site?

BECKY: He showed me one and said, "You just fill out the application and that's all there is to it."

JUDITH: Well, if you want my two cents, I wouldn't like to meet anyone that way.

DAISY: Face to face without any faces? I wouldn't want to meet any man unless I could look him in the eye.

JUDITH: Don't you think we're too <u>old</u> to be dating?

BECKY: Okay. I got it. Let's change the subject. You used to drink wine like the rest of us. Why the Vodka lately?

JUDITH: Well, I read that Vodka can increase blood-flow and circulation in your body which can prevent clots, strokes,

Act I - Scene 1

and other heart diseases. Vodka can also help lower your cholesterol, <u>and</u>...there's only 64 calories in a glass.

DAISY: My God! It's healthier than a smoothie! Thanks, professor. Should we be taking notes?

BECKY: Judith, how was your Thanksgiving? Are you still killing yourself to do the whole dinner?

JUDITH: No, thank God. This year everyone brought a dish. All I had to do was cook the turkey and set things up. Oh, and clean up after they all left.

DAISY: Hallelulah!

JUDITH: Dinner was great. Everyone had a wonderful time. Even Maxwell had fun. He couldn't stop laughing. What a clown! Everything seemed to tickle his funny bone.

DAISY: When someone is in good spirits, look for the good spirits! [Beat]

[Judith gives Daisy a puzzled look]

BECKY: Not having Jacob and Mason here for Thanksgiving was a real downer. I miss them.

DAISY: You shouldn't be surprised that they couldn't get away at this time of year.

Widows At The Club

BECKY: I know. Of course, this is when department stores make their money, but I sure did miss having them at my house for a day or two. It was quiet and lonely and boring.

DAISY: If they worked at your department store, would you be eager to give them time off?

BECKY: I suppose you're right. With all the year-end sales and promotions, I need all the help I can get.

DAISY: Bet you're a regular slave driver every year at this time.

BECKY: I can still dream, can't I?

DAISY: Dreams aren't reality, and reality is not a dream. Wow! Sometimes I impress myself! Deep thoughts from Daisy. [Beat]

BECKY: You can't tell me that you don't get lonely these days. Can you?

DAISY: The house does get pretty quiet with everyone gone, but I still have Heather and her kids nearby. I can go to her house and listen to the TV or the latest argument between her and her useless husband if I'm hungering for noise.

BECKY: I get noise all day at the store, but when I get home, I have no one to talk to. When I was the furniture buyer,

Act I - Scene 1

Hershel and I decided that I should use my maiden name. Since no one knew I was the owner's wife, ...

DAISY: Oh, so you were Hershel's spy in the store!

BECKY: Well, you might call me that. I'll tell you it made for interesting conversation once Hershel came home.

DAISY: At least he came home!

BECKY: Now, I have no one to share the excitement of my day. Yeah, I do get lonely since he's gone.

DAISY: I get lonely, too, since the schmuck is gone. But that doesn't mean I want to meet a man. I still think all men are useless.

JUDITH: I sure could have used Archie when I had to clean the kitchen after everyone went home. The house was so quiet. And I did feel the loneliness. I must confess, I actually poured myself a glass of vodka.

BECKY: Vodka? The silence must have been overwhelming!

DAISY: So, my daughter is contemplating dumping her worthless husband and you want me to have fun finding a man. Becky, you must be crazy to think I would be interested.

Widows At The Club

JUDITH: I don't know when I'll ever be ready for another man in my life.

BECKY: Are you saying you don't think this would be fun?

JUDITH: I'm not looking for fun in that way. I know I would never be able to replace my Archie.

BECKY: Are you two trying to say you don't want to meet anyone?

DAISY: How did you guess?

BECKY: Well, I'm still curious. I want to see what it's like. Why can't we just pretend? You know, just check it out? We don't actually have to go out on a date.

JUDITH: Okay, I'll agree to play your game, but you know I'm not interested.

BECKY: We can pretend and still check out some dating sites.

DAISY: Becky, you're not giving up on this, are you?

BECKY: I'm not giving up on something that we haven't even tried yet.

Act I - Scene 1

JUDITH: Okay, okay, you've made your point. I've got a computer, so I'll volunteer to check a few things out and I will even bring notes next week.

DAISY: I think we've just proven that we're never too old to learn something <u>stupid</u>! [Beat]

JUDITH: I'm getting hungry. I think I'm going to have a personal pizza, tonight.

DAISY: I'm in the mood for a burger and fries. I'll work it off at pickleball, tomorrow.

BECKY: I think I'll have the mixed pair: Soup and Salad.

DAISY: There you go, again! Still pairing yourself up!

[Lights down and girls exit stage.]

End of Scene 1 – Act I

Act I - Scene 2

Second Week of December at the Club

[The ladies take seats. Daisy's back needs to be to the entrance. Becky raises her hand and circles her wrist to indicate that their drinks can be delivered.]

BECKY: It looks like Judith's late again ... as usual. I wonder what her excuse is this week.

DAISY: Maybe she got tied up teaching knot-making to girl scouts. [Beat] Did you get a chance to read Judith's Christmas newsletter?

BECKY: I did. ... It sounded like it was written by a professional novelist.

DAISY: Well, what would you expect from a retired English teacher?

BECKY: Talk about perfect ... every word and description sounded like the perfect family. Do you believe that anyone's family can be that perfect? Oy, I should be so lucky!

Widows At The Club

Her grandson made the football team, another one got tapped for National Honor Society, and she wrote about the cruise she took them on.

DAISY: Her Christmas newsletter sure did sound as though she was living in a perfect world. We know it's not all sunshine and roses! What about that no-good grandson, Maxwell...the one who's always in trouble because of drugs? [Judith enters.] Don't you remember when he got picked up?

[Judith is still bundled up for winter.]

JUDITH: Hi girls, who got picked up?

DAISY: Uh ... I was just telling Becky that ... some young girl that I golf with was ... telling me ... that her brother just got picked up by a gal that he barely knows.

[Judith stands behind her chair.]

JUDITH: Hmmm. These girls today. ... So brazen. [Purse hits table.]

BECKY: Judith, you're late again. What's your excuse this time?

[Judith is telling them why she is late while she is taking off her gloves, scarf and coat. She continues standing until she finishes her story.]

Act I - Scene 2

JUDITH: Well, I was late because I had to get gas. It was one fiasco after another. First, I didn't go to my regular station. I had to get out of the car to put my credit card in and I remembered that I forgot to reach under my steering wheel to open the gas tank. So, I got back in the car and pulled the lever. Then I got out again and put my credit card into the slot and the machine wanted my zip code. Honestly, I almost forgot my own zip code.

Well, I got through that hurdle and the next thing I know, it was telling me I have to pay inside. By this time, I had not pumped any gas and my hands were already freezing because I needed to take off my gloves to put the credit card into the slot and "remove quickly."

So, I tried again, and it still said I had to pay inside. Hmmm. I went inside, gave the cashier my credit card and said, "I want to fill up my gas tank and that pump seems to not understand me." The attendant said, "You can't do a fill up on your credit card. ... We can only put in a specified amount." By this time, I'm getting frustrated, but I said, "Okay, ... give me $20.00 worth of gas."

He ran my card through for $20.00 worth of gas and out I went into the cold to squeeze the pump for my gas. At least at this point I had my gloves back on ... and ... [Judith sits, exhausted.] and that's why I'm late.

[Prop person delivers drinks. Ladies acknowledge.]

Widows At The Club

BECKY: Oy, I remember when you could pull up to a gas station and tell the attendant how much gas you wanted, and he would pump the gas for you. He also would clean your windshield, check your oil, and check your tires for air. And he did it with a smile. Yes sirree, all while I stayed in my warm car. My how things have changed.

DAISY: Yep, that's the name of the game these days. Change. Change. Change. And they call that progress?

JUDITH: I remember how hard it was to roll down the windows in my brother's car – especially when the crank fell off in my hand.

BECKY: Yes, that was before automatic windows. I remember my parents' car had side vent windows. When I first learned to drive, my smoking friends used to hang their cigarettes out those little triangular windows.

JUDITH: Why do you suppose we all thought smoking was so cool?

DAISY: I don't know, it just was.

JUDITH: Even Archie and I got hooked as teenagers. He never was able to kick the habit.

BECKY: Maybe it was our way to rebel against our parents. Who knew it was bad for our health?

Act I - Scene 2

JUDITH: Back then, people weren't saying smoking was bad for us. If they had told us it would cause lung cancer, maybe Archie would have quit before it was too late.

DAISY: Daddy told me NO SMOKING in his car. Not for health reasons. He just didn't like the smell. So, on Friday nights when I had his car, it was a pain to tell my friends not to smoke.

JUDITH: My friends and I used to cruise the drive-in restaurant, and everybody chipped in 10 cents each to gas up the car.

BECKY: I think gas was about 30 cents a gallon back then.

JUDITH: Isn't it funny that we can remember how much a gallon of gas cost years ago, but I had a hard time remembering my zip code today?

DAISY: Maybe those really were the good old days.

BECKY: You got that right. Seems like everything is self-serve these days. When I pull up to an ATM machine, I have to get out of my car just to reach the buttons, so ... I have decided to do things the old-fashioned way. I park my car at the bank and go inside to do my banking. And ... I get to deal with a real person ... not a machine.

DAISY: What a concept!

Widows At The Club

JUDITH: Yes, it does seem as though everything is becoming self-serve these days.

DAISY: Riiight. Even the grocery store is phasing out traditional service. They want you to use the self-serve checkout counter and bag your own groceries and they have the nerve to tell you that this is for your convenience.

JUDITH: Convenience? How can they get away with that?

BECKY: I think they're just beginning to brainwash us for the day when there will be NO MORE cashiers. Self-serve all the way. And they want us to think this is progress. Our customers love the small store feel of Goldstein's compared to the big chain department stores. Personal service and a familiarity with the customers is why they keep coming back.

DAISY: I liked those good old days when the cashier checked out my groceries and the bagger bagged 'em... and a real person pumped my gas.

BECKY: I agree. And, the bag boys always carried your groceries to the car. Speaking of checking out, did you check out dating sites like you said you would last week?

JUDITH: Yes, I looked up dating sites, just like I promised. I even wrote down several profile questions from a few of them.

Act I - Scene 2

BECKY: [To Daisy.] I guess everything is an open book on the internet.

DAISY: How would I know? I've never owned a computer!

BECKY: You may be the last hold-out!

DAISY: Well, I've got news for you. Heather just told me they were buying me a laptop computer for Christmas.

JUDITH: It's about time.

DAISY: I told her not to waste her money. I've gotten along without one, so why would I want one of those stupid machines, at this time of my life. I told Heather you can't teach an old-dog-new-tricks. She said, "Don't worry Mom, the kids are excited to teach you how to use it.

JUDITH: That's how I learned. All of my grandchildren taught me a little at a time, when they were at my house.

BECKY: That's one reason why I bonded so well with Zack these past few years.

DAISY: If my grandchildren are willing to teach a "tech-tard" like me to use a computer, I just might have a chance to bond with them. Wouldn't that be a change?

Widows At The Club

BECKY: Zack loved showing me how to date online. This really could be fun.

DAISY: We never decided to do anything for real. We were sort of pretending if I recall.

BECKY: Okay, okay! So, we're just going to pretend. Judith, what did you find?

JUDITH: I copied a few of the profile questions I found on E-Symphony, and assuming you might be interested in a Jewish man, I copied some questions from a site called *J Men Only*. So, you girls can have fun answering them.

BECKY: Judith, I know you weren't very interested in this, but we kind of talked about all of us giving it a try.

JUDITH: You're half right...I never said I was interested. I only said I would check out a few of these sites for the two of you.

BECKY: It will be a lot more interesting if we all get involved. Did you find that Jewish site I mentioned called *Rent-A-Yenta dot com*?

JUDITH: Yes.

BECKY: Good! Zack and I scouted other sites that were just for seniors, and he seriously encouraged me to follow through. I

Act I - Scene 2

guess he seems to think I need to meet a man. Come to think of it, even my rabbi suggested a man I might like to meet.

JUDITH: No one seems to think I need to meet a man. Archie has been dead less than two years. My family would be horrified!

BECKY: Two years may feel like a short time. We know your sense of loss still hurts, but you can't put your life on hold forever!

DAISY: Your pain is still fresh. We miss him, too. But it *has* been almost two years.

JUDITH: Oh, all right, I suppose I could help you look over these questions.

BECKY: Yes. That sounds like a good idea. How about you, Daisy?

DAISY: [She rolls her eyes.] Sure ... Why not?

BECKY: I already started answering some questions at home. [Becky removes a paper from her purse.] This could be our example.

DAISY: That's great, Becky. As usual, you are leading us by the nose.

JUDITH: It doesn't really matter to me because I'm probably not going to send this thing in anyway.

DAISY: Look at this one. It asks for my name, age, and occupation. Since I have only been the "perfect housewife" all my life, how would I answer the question of occupation?

JUDITH: Well, you know, I would have no problem with that question. I'll just say, "Retired schoolteacher."

BECKY: I would simply say I was a furniture buyer in a Department Store.

DAISY: Why not say you <u>own</u> the store?

BECKY: I don't want a man who would want me for my money. You've heard the old saying, at our age a man only wants a woman for a nurse and a purse. [Beat]

DAISY: Yeah, I've heard that expression, too. [Daisy nods her head and slowly repeats.] A nurse and a purse.

BECKY: We've got to think about what we want to reveal to a stranger who might be interested in us.

DAISY: It might be easy for the two of you, but I married the schmuck right after high school and never had a job in my life. Do I just say, "Occupation: housewife and mother?"

Act I - Scene 2

I can't imagine any man wanting to take out a woman who was only a "housewife and mother."

JUDITH: Well, that might be <u>exactly</u> what a man wants!

BECKY: Could be. How would you respond to this question? "The one I am looking for would be _____."

JUDITH: That would be easy for me. If I ever went on one of these dating sites, I would be looking for a man just like my Archie.

DAISY: Like I said, we miss him, too. But I don't think that's the answer they're looking for. I'm sure they wouldn't want to hear about your Archie.

BECKY: You're right. ... I filled that out by saying I wanted a man who likes fine dining and fine wines. I think that alludes to expensive restaurants and expensive wines ... and if a guy tests positive in those categories, I might assume he has money.

DAISY: Wow, Becky, you put a lot of thought into this! I never would have been that sneaky.

JUDITH: That's not sneaky, Daisy. That's clever!

BECKY: Thanks, Judith. We need to be clever with our answers.

Widows At The Club

JUDITH: Since Archie said he would never cook but he would clean the kitchen when *I* cooked, does that mean that I can't say, "The one I'm looking for would be a dishwasher"?

DAISY: Are you saying you're looking for a machine?

JUDITH: You know what I mean, Daisy; someone to help with the dishes.

BECKY: Let's see. You might say ... "I'm looking for a man who enjoys spending time in the kitchen."

JUDITH: Clever enough.

DAISY: Well, Mr. Schmuck never spent much time with me, let alone helping out in the kitchen.

JUDITH: Do you think he did that kind of thing with his girlfriend?

BECKY: I doubt it.

DAISY: So, if I were to describe the one *I'm* looking for, the "unclever" way would be to say, "I am looking for a monogamous man."

JUDITH: Could you even find a man who can pronounce monogamous?

Act I - Scene 2

DAISY: Could you find a man who wouldn't choke on that word? [Beat]

BECKY: But what would you say to get the answer you're looking for?

JUDITH: Could you say, "I'm looking for a one-woman man"?

BECKY: Too obvious.

DAISY: Or should I say, "I'm looking for a guy who would only have eyes for me."

BECKY: Too obvious.

JUDITH: Well, how would you describe a monogamous man?

BECKY: Hmmm. I never thought of that. Maybe there's no way to get that answer on a piece of paper.

DAISY: I think if you ever asked a question like that, *ALL* men would lie.

JUDITH: So, since we can't weed out the cheaters ... what can we say we want?

DAISY: Okay, I think I've got the answer. I think I'll just say it the way it is. I want a man who will always be honest.

Widows At The Club

BECKY: I can't think of a better way, Daisy. ... Judith, what do you think you would be looking for at this stage of your life, **IF** you were really going to fill out an application?

JUDITH: Just a man like Archie.

BECKY: [The two of them groan] You're no help.

DAISY: Hey, I am going to get serious about what kind of a man I would look for. He would have to be adventurous, kind, and ... *MONOGAMOUS*.

JUDITH and BECKY: Come on Daisy,

BECKY: We have just been over that.

DAISY: Okay, I'm looking for a man who will always be true, adventurous, kind and [Blurts out.] TALL, DARK, AND HANDSOME.

JUDITH and BECKY: DAISY!

DAISY: Okay, how about this? I'm looking for a man who will always be honest, adventurous, kind and loves going to the theater. Oh, and he must enjoy golf.

BECKY: That's more like it! Judith, what kind of man are you looking for?

Act I - Scene 2

JUDITH: A man like Archie.

BECKY and DAISY: *JUDITH*!

JUDITH: Okay. My guy should be courteous, kind, funny, loves spending time in the kitchen. Loves bridge and he must be reliable. How's that?

BECKY: That ought to do it, Judith.

DAISY: I agree. Sounds like you just recited the Boy Scout Oath! The kind of man an English teacher would be looking for.

JUDITH: The next question is asking us to "**describe yourself in 30 words or less**." [Judith looks around the table.] Anyone have any ideas?

BECKY: That could be more difficult than it sounds.

[Lights down and girls exit stage.]

End of Scene 2 – Act I

Act I - Scene 3

Third Week of December at the Club

[Enter Daisy and Becky. Daisy sits with her back to the entrance.] [No drink order. No drinks.]

BECKY: Less than a week till Christmas. My store is really busy. I hope you were able to find what you needed before it's too late.

DAISY: I'm all set. Just have to finish wrapping.

BECKY: Oh, my! What a lovely Christmas sweater! I'm struck speechless by its beauty!

DAISY: You're right! I should turn it into an evening gown for all the fancy balls I get invited to!

BECKY: Touché! Did you ever get invited to bring a plus-one to your numerous fancy balls?

DAISY: What? What's a plus-one?

Widows At The Club

BECKY: That's when a couple's event comes with an invitation to a single person to allow them to bring a companion.

DAISY Thank GOD I've never needed a plus-one.

BECKY: Well, my friend Ruth is on the dinner dance fundraiser at the Temple and she told me I should come. I told her I was uncomfortable going to a dance of any kind alone and she said just bring a plus-one.

DAISY: Puleeze. I have no need for a plus-one. But...thanks for the beautiful compliment on my sweater. You know, I have sweaters for all the holidays.

BECKY: I have a Hanukkah sweater. Not as special as this, but nice.

DAISY: I've never seen one of those in the stores. Where did you get it?

BECKY: I didn't buy it. My daughter bought it for me a couple years ago and I remember asking where she got it. She said Zack found it online and Rivka bought it on Amazon.

DAISY: These kids. They buy everything online! Online, online, why does everything have to be online? I have never bought anything that way. I don't feel comfortable buying something that I can't see in person, or touch, or try on. And now, you want us to buy a man online!

Act I - Scene 3

BECKY: That's the new way, Daisy. That's how everything's done these days. Yes, even dating is done online.

DAISY: Makes me feel a little old.

BECKY: Speaking of that, [Hold up papers.] *Rent-a-Yenta.com* asked, "In a nutshell - describe yourself."

DAISY: Nutshell? Are we the squirrels or are we the nuts for letting you guide us in this "adventure?" Either way, we're nuts.

BECKY: Your objections are over the top. What are you really afraid of?

DAISY: If I actually went on a date, the thing I would most fear would be letting him hear me **fart**!

BECKY: Oh, come on. Be honest with me.

DAISY: Think about it. When a man farts, he thinks it's funny. But women aren't supposed to fart. We're too delicate or perfect or something.

BECKY: You've got a point, but that's really superficial. I'm not buying it.

DAISY: Don't laugh at me, but I think I'm afraid of being rejected. You'd think that living with Mr. Schmuck would make me immune to rejection, but he didn't really push me away.

He just became my grumpy brother who looked elsewhere for love.

BECKY: Yes, that would hurt, but think of the benefits if you found a good man.

DAISY: I've been without a husband for ten years and I've found a way to deal with car breakdowns, toilet clogs, and furnace repairs.

BECKY: Men are good for more than repairs. A true companion might find ways to make you feel good. Good enough to be worth the occasional rejection.

DAISY: Just between you and me, ... I do still have dreams.

BECKY: That's the spirit. Don't you think we're all afraid of rejection?

DAISY: Don't tell Judith, but I am curious about this new way to meet people. [Beat] So long as we don't get ourselves in trouble.

BECKY: So, did you look at any of this? [Hold up papers.]

DAISY: I didn't want to get ahead of you two, so I decided to wait until we were all together for this. It'll be interesting to hear if Judith spent any time on this.

Act I - Scene 3

BECKY: She's probably still stuck on wanting someone just like Archie.

DAISY: When she married him, she got lucky and really did win the lottery!

[Judith enters.]

JUDITH: Who won the lottery?

DAISY: You did.

JUDITH: What are you talking about?

DAISY: We were just saying you must have won the lottery and spent time at the store picking up all that cash, so that must be why you're late. I suppose you'll probably be late for your own funeral.

JUDITH: What would that be like? Being late for my own funeral! Come to think of it, when I read the paper with my morning coffee, the obit page is the first thing I read. Remember that red-head I used to golf with? She just died and she was only 72.

BECKY: Oy, let's not talk about funerals. It seems like people we know are dropping like flies these days. Life isn't getting any longer for us. We should be thinking about how much more we would like to do while we're still alive.

DAISY: Yes, I guess I'll have to agree with you on that.

JUDITH: I brought the paperwork you mentioned last week. You remember, that site asked us to "describe yourself in 30 words or less."

DAISY: 30 words or less...in a nutshell...this is really starting to get complicated.

BECKY: It's the same question, just worded differently. So, how would you describe yourself, Daisy?

DAISY: Hmmm, a Ph.D. in cake baking, a Master's degree in dusting, a Bachelor's degree in taking out the trash!

BECKY: I can see you're fighting me on this! You haven't got a serious bone in your body.

DAISY: If we can't have fun doing this, why do it? You did say it would be fun.

JUDITH: It doesn't matter. We're just pretending.

BECKY: I'll have to admit, it is getting a little tricky. [Beat]

JUDITH: Did you think answering these personal questions would be so difficult?

BECKY: Oh? Personal questions?

Act I - Scene 3

JUDITH: You know...like the body type question.

BECKY: I don't know how I would answer that question.

DAISY: I think they're asking if you are <u>FAT</u>.

JUDITH: Why do they have to ask such personal questions? Do I say my body is sexy when I don't think my body is sexy?

DAISY: What's sexy for a polar bear may not be sexy for a gazelle. [Beat]

BECKY: Remember girls, the men have to answer the same questions.

DAISY: How else can you decide who you're willing to waste an entire evening with? Don't you think everyone lies when filling out these profiles.

BECKY: I think I could shave a few years off my age and maybe a few pounds off my weight. The hard part would be remembering what year I was born.

JUDITH: Do you think we should do that? Hey, wait a minute...we're not really doing this. We're just pretending to do this. So, what difference does it make what we say?

BECKY: I'd like to see what we would be saying if we were not pretending.

Widows At The Club

JUDITH: Okay, let's try being honest. That's what my Archie would do.

[Pause while the girls look over more questions.]

JUDITH: Becky, what did you think of that dating site for Jewish matchmaking?

DAISY: So...what's it called... *Latke Lovers dot com*?

BECKY: It should be called "Match Making with a Mensch".

JUDITH: A mensch is good, right?

DAISY: Yeah, mensch is Jewish for that fictional man who is everything good and pure. He's a regular Jesus Christ!

BECKY: Okay. Enough with the jokes! Let's get serious. Let's see where these questions lead us... just to see how it goes.

DAISY: Really Becky, I'm not in the market for a new man. Are you angling for us to sign up for real? Would you actually sign up with one of those Jewish dating sites?

BECKY: I might.

JUDITH: I think we should all pretend to sign up with a different one and then we can compare notes. Let's say Becky signs up for *J-Matchmakers dot com* or *Synagogue Singles*

Act I - Scene 3

for Seniors. I would be willing to fill out a form for *e-Symphony.*

BECKY: Okay, I think I'll check out *Rent-A-Yenta*. That sounds like my speed. Daisy, you could look at *Play-It-Again-Sam dot com* or *Partners in Time.*

DAISY: Are you sure we should really do this?

BECKY: Sure, why not? We can sign up, but we don't have to go on any real dates. It'll be fun to see where this goes!

End of Scene 3 – Act I

Act I - Scene 4

First Week of January at the Club

[All three girls enter.] [Becky raises her hand and circles her wrist to indicate that their drinks can be delivered.]

BECKY: I hope you all had a great holiday. As for me, I was D & D on New Year's Eve. It was very lonely.

JUDITH: What's D & D, Becky?

BECKY: Zach told me it means Desperate and Dateless.

DAISY: Speak for yourself, Becky. I was dateless but I never thought of myself as desperate. I did my usual. … I watched the ball come down at midnight in Time's Square.

JUDITH: Me, too. But I fell asleep before the ball came down.

BECKY: Don't be too hard on yourself. Being alone changes the meaning of every special occasion, and without Archie there, it's no wonder you fell asleep. I spent my New Year's

Widows At The Club

Eve in the same way as you two... and I'm really getting tired of doing this every year alone.

JUDITH: The Holidays are always wonderful with my brood but by the time the ball comes down there is a sense of emptiness. Daisy, didn't you feel that, too?

DAISY: I guess.

JUDITH: How long did it take for holidays to stop being bittersweet?

BECKY: I still miss Hershel, but the intensity of emotion does get less with the passage of time. So, Daisy, how was your Christmas?

DAISY: Christmas was okay on my end. They did get me that stupid computer and ... Heather made a few hints to me that there may be a divorce coming.

JUDITH: You know as Catholics; we're not allowed to get divorced.

DAISY: Thank God, we're not Catholic! What could be worse than a lifetime sentence to Hell?!

BECKY: I think being without the companionship of a man for the rest of my life might be like a sentence to Hell.

Act I - Scene 4

JUDITH: I sure do miss my Archie.

[Daisy pats Judith's hand. Becky opens purse and brings out papers.]

BECKY: So, did any of you find time to work on these questions?

DAISY: I started to look mine over, but I'm beginning to think my daughter is the one who needs this more than me.

BECKY: She's still married, Daisy, and you're not.

[Prop person delivers drinks. Ladies ad lib.]

JUDITH: You know, I actually learned some things about myself while thinking about these questions.

DAISY: I know all I want to know about myself. Maybe a little too much.

BECKY: You can never know too much about yourself.

DAISY: I look in the mirror and I see the beginnings of an old lady, complete with wrinkles, saggy skin, dark spots, and grey roots. But I don't **_feel_** I'm any older than I was twenty years ago. And then I think about all my aches and pains. ... I really am getting older!

Widows At The Club

JUDITH: We all feel that way, Daisy.

DAISY: But I don't want to know that. I want to live in ignorance and believe that my best years are ahead of me. I want to believe I can still shave more strokes off my handicap and still knock 'em dead in a two-piece bathing suit! {Alternative line: ... and maybe a couple of pounds off my athletic build.}

BECKY: Face it. Those days are gone.

JUDITH: There's nothing we can do about it.

BECKY: I'm sure most men would find you very attractive.

DAISY: It still sucks!

BECKY: I think we'd all feel better if we knew we could still attract a man. I wonder if we ever finish an application, would we really send them in?

JUDITH: I guess I could send one in, but I still don't think I would go on an actual date.

BECKY: Daisy, you might actually meet a man who would treat you right.

JUDITH: They are out there. After all, look at my Archie. He was a saint of a man!

Act I - Scene 4

BECKY: Did you work on your description of yourself?

DAISY: I sure did.

BECKY: Let's hear it.

DAISY: I see the world as it really is. Good golfer. Nice head of hair, (Hey, I'm not bald yet.) athletic build, two grown children and two grandchildren. Learning to play Pickleball, love to cook.

BECKY: Much better!

JUDITH: What do you mean by "the world as it really is?"

DAISY: It means the world really sucks.

BECKY: Daisy! What man would want a woman who thinks the world sucks?

DAISY: What woman would want a man when all men suck?

JUDITH: I told you, my Archie was a wonderful man. Unfortunately, you've only been with a bad one. ... There are plenty of good men out there.

DAISY: Yeah, riiiight...name one. Oh, other than Archie.

JUDITH: Most of the men Archie and I knew were really nice.

BECKY: There are good guys and bad guys out there. You just have to give this thing a try.

JUDITH: You're perfect for this, Daisy. You would know how to recognize the bad ones, so you won't get fooled again.

DAISY: It's easy to be fooled. Men are like sheets, when you're wrapped up in them, it's easy to get disoriented and difficult to get out. Shopping for sheets can be confusing, too. I remember looking at a set of sheets a few months ago and it is the same price now during the white sale as it was two months ago when it wasn't on sale.

JUDITH: Wow! I don't know how you got from men to sheets so fast!

DAISY: Nothing makes sense when you're shopping for men or sheets.

BECKY: Well, a department store doesn't necessarily lower the price on everything when they advertise a sale. ... Sometimes this business is overwhelming –

DAISY: Like dealing with men.

BECKY: Let me finish! Overwhelming - especially during the holiday season and the end of year sales period. The stores at the mall are very worried about their bottom line.

Act I - Scene 4

DAISY: If I went on a date with a man, I'd be worried about my bottom, too!

JUDITH: Eew! Let's change the subject!

DAISY: Okay. Becky, what did you say about yourself?

BECKY: Just for fun, I looked up pinot grigio on my computer and I got a description that fits me to a "T." It said, "A Pinot Grigio lover is charming and attractive. You love romance, excitement, and tend to always be looking forward to your next adventure. As a socialite, you adore meeting new people and have a spontaneous side. Although you can be gullible at times, you always manage to find your way out of a sticky situation!"

JUDITH: That was a description of the kind of person who drinks Pinot Grigio?

BECKY: I got that right off the internet!

DAISY: That sounds like more than 30 words.

BECKY: On *Rent-A-Yenta* they don't limit me to 30 words. They only say to describe yourself "in a nutshell."

DAISY: So, now you're "in a nutshell?"

JUDITH: You never mentioned whether these sites charge for their services.

BECKY: Zack said, "There is a cost Grandma. It's about one hundred dollars to join, plus some hidden additional charges." He did say there is one site that is free called *Play-It-Again-Sam dot com*.

JUDITH: Sounds like that's the one I might choose, because it's free ... if I were doing this for real.

BECKY: Okay, Daisy, so tell us what dating site you might consider.

DAISY: I thought about *E-Symphony* and I also looked closely at *Partners-In-Time*. That is **IF** I were to fill out an application.

BECKY: So, you're already using your new computer, my dear. How did you manage that?

DAISY: My granddaughter taught me to Google and she also taught me how to play solitaire. Oh, I'm just a thoroughly modern Daisy.

JUDITH: Good for you! You're on your way. ... Oh Becky, what did you mean by "hidden additional costs?"

BECKY: Well, I'm not sure exactly, but Zack told me that they might charge you a small monthly fee over and above

Act I - Scene 4

what you initially pay to join ... just for the privilege of seeing what men are looking at your profile.

JUDITH: Are you kidding? You have to pay more money just to see who is reading your profile. Makes me glad I'm looking at a free site.

DAISY: I can tell you right now ... I would not want to pay any extra to see who's looking at me. I still think this whole thing is a waste of time.

BECKY: Daisy, you're just saying that because your husband was such a schmuck.

JUDITH: So, Becky, what do you hope to find from this adventure?

BECKY: I don't have much time for a man in my life right now because of all the hours I have to spend at the store; however, I am hoping to change that. I have hopes of finding a companion and a theater buddy and a Saturday night date all rolled up in one.

DAISY: Sounds to me like you are really getting serious about this project. What about you Judith?

JUDITH: <u>Wwelll,</u> ... once I got started, I just kept going. How about you?

Widows At The Club

BECKY: It's beginning to look like we all still have a lot of work to do.

JUDITH: Let's come back to this next week.

DAISY: Becky, I've been hesitant to bring this up because I know it's going to upset you, but I heard a story about online dating that really scares me. Heather has a friend whose widowed mother met this guy online and fell head over heels in love with him. Apparently, they tried a couple of times to meet up and something always got in the way. But they were having a torrid love affair by e-mails.

BECKY: So, she fell in love with his e-mails. Is that such a terrible thing?

DAISY: The story gets better, or worse I should say.

JUDITH: What could be better than love letters? My parents fell in love writing love letters during the war. It's so romantic!

DAISY: Well, apparently this guy got stuck overseas in order to finish up a government contract. He said he needed a small loan to tide him over until his job was finished and then he could finally settle up some personal things and fly here, so he could hold her in his arms.

BECKY: What's wrong with that?

Act I - Scene 4

DAISY: Becky, you're not getting the whole story. Heather told me her friend's mother started sending him money on a regular basis. Soon she realized she was into him for about $100,000.00 before she woke up to the fact that she was being scammed. I don't know all the details, but we should be scared and leery of being scammed.

JUDITH: Wow. I wonder if I would ever be able to recognize a scam like that. I remember when Mother passed away, I was going through her things and found all of Daddy's love letters to her. How could any man ruin such a wonderful thing?

DAISY: All men are scum. I'm glad we're only pretending.

BECKY: I'm sure your story is one in a million.

JUDITH: But what could keep that from happening to us?

End of Scene 4 - Act I

15 Minute Intermission

Act 2 - Scene 5

Second Week of January at the Club

[Judith enters and sits before lights up.] [Curtain up and lights on as Daisy enters.]

DAISY: What? No story about transporting your granddaughter's basketball team to Outer Mongolia for chicken wings?

JUDITH: Don't faint Daisy.

DAISY: Miracle of miracles.

JUDITH: I'm trying to be on time more often. You know it's a New Year's resolution that I probably won't be able to keep. Did you spend any time on your "profile questions" last week?

DAISY: Are you kidding? My week was full. Went to the Y...exercised with Silver Sneakers, did water aerobics and played pickleball. It's a lot cheaper than golf since I'm using my "Silver Sneakers" membership. I'm staying in shape, and learning to enjoy another sport during the winter months.

JUDITH: "Silver Sneakers?" Don't you think that gives away your age?

DAISY: What do you want to call it? "Golden Tennis Shoes?"

JUDITH: Golden? As in "Golden-agers?" You're saying we're old no matter how you say it. In any case, I know what you mean. I used to enjoy skiing with Archie and the kids in the winter but... now that the kids are grown, and Archie is gone ... I guess there's nothing left for me to enjoy on a cold winter day but to **snuggle in bed under the covers ...** [Becky hurries in.]

BECKY: Who's in bed under the covers?

[Becky raises her hand and circles her wrist to indicate that their drinks can be delivered.]

DAISY: Oh, Becky, get a grip. Ever since we started talking about this computer match-making thing you seem to have nothing else on your mind.

BECKY: Maybe you're right. Last week when you shared that story about scammers, I really got worried. I found out that there are clues to recognizing a scammer. We can still do this, and we can help each other NOT get scammed.

Act 2 - Scene 5

JUDITH: How do you propose we help each other?

BECKY: I looked up online dating scammers and Daisy was right. They are really out there, but they all seem to follow a pattern. If someone starts writing and falling in love very fast, that should be a red flag. And if they are far away so it's inconvenient to meet in person, that should be a red flag, too. We could warn each other.

DAISY: All the more reason why I wouldn't like to date. It's like a job interview for a gig that I may not want. Eventually, you will learn that all jobs suck in some way. Better to be alone than stuck with bad company.

JUDITH: Daisy, Becky just assured us that we can help each other and right away you bad mouth dating. Even just pretending, you are negative.

BECKY: As I was saying...there are other signs of scamming. Like broken promises to visit you and a need for an emergency loan. Here, I made this list so we can all be on the lookout for these scams.

DAISY: I told you men were all scum.

BECKY: If we all do this together, we can avoid those scumbags.

Widows At The Club

JUDITH: I suppose this list will make me feel a little better. Now, let's hear why <u>you're</u> late this time!

BECKY: Nothing of importance. I was helping a friend go over her belongings for her neighborhood garage sale in the spring because she's starting to consider downsizing. The time just got away from me. I rushed home to shower and change and here I am.

DAISY: Downsizing. I have thought about that from time to time, but I'm not ready for my final move.

BECKY: What do you mean ... final move. When I think of a final move, I think of a place that's six feet under.

DAISY: Just because you have a cozy condo for one doesn't mean that the rest of us are in your shoes. Look at Judith. She's living in a house that at one time housed four kids and a husband.

JUDITH: That's right!

BECKY: Maybe you could call it right-sizing, Judith. Certainly, that big house is not right for you now that Archie and the kids are gone.

JUDITH: I wouldn't know where to begin to get rid of my things. I still have the kid's bedrooms filled with all their things pretty much as it was when they went off to college.

Act 2 - Scene 5

BECKY: Judith, you're a perfect candidate for right-sizing. Why would anyone want to take care of that big house ... and all that stuff that's in it?

JUDITH: It would take me a year of garage sales to rid myself of everything that I would need to sell or give away to get into a smaller place.

BECKY: Please, don't ask for my help.

JUDITH: I have asked my kids a million times to take what they want out of their rooms, and they just say ..." You keep it for me, Mom....You have more room in your house than I have." [Judith sighs.] I still have all of their old high school yearbooks and the girls' prom dresses are still hanging in their closets. Come to think of it ... I have my son's tennis trophies and his high school letter jacket still in his room where he left them.

DAISY: Well, how thoughtful of them!

JUDITH: I don't think I could ever downsize.

[Prop person delivers drinks. Ladies ad lib.]

BECKY: I'll tell you this. I love my little condo overlooking our golf course. If the roof leaks the association takes care of it ... I never have to shovel snow or mow grass. I don't know how you can sleep at night in that big old house with all the things that could go wrong, especially since Archie is gone.

JUDITH: Yes. He was my very handy "handy man."

DAISY: Downsizing? I still have the sterling silver that was given to me and the schmuck at our wedding. I haven't used it in a hundred years and who in the hell would ever want to polish it up for use even if I had an occasion to use it.

BECKY: Why don't you give it to your daughter?

DAISY: Yeah. Riiiight. Her no "good nick" husband barely has a job, so when would she ever serve dinner with sterling silver? I think most of their fine dining at home revolves around pizza and take out Chinese. And, I don't have any sterling silver chopsticks.

JUDITH: Now, that's fine dining!

DAISY: Actually, I have considered downsizing but where would I go? I don't want to make more than one move and I am definitely not ready for one of those four step apartments ... You know, Independent Living, Assisted Living, Memory Care, and finally Skilled nursing. Ugh! And ... when I had lunch with my friend who recently moved into *Serenity Park for Seniors,* I noticed a whole bunch of walkers and wheelchairs. Nope, not ready for that.

Act 2 - Scene 5

BECKY: I love the carefree life I have living in my condo. The only right-sizing I'm doing is trying to sell my sterling silver. I offered it ... service for twelve - - to my grandson and he said, "Grandma, what would I do with that?" "But Zack," I said. I think it's worth a lot of money!" [Everyone nods.] He quickly googled e-Bay, you know, that auction company on the computer. He looked up something similar to my sterling and it went for about $3,000.

JUDITH: Wow!

BECKY: He turned down something that might be worth $3,000, so I asked him, "What am I supposed to do with this silverware? It even comes in a beautiful wood box!" He said, "Grandma, you should auction it off on e-Bay and get what you can for it."

DAISY: Maybe Zack could teach an old "silver-sneaker" like me how to sell *MY* silver.

BECKY: Let me get this straight, Judith. Your kids are not willing to help you downsize and your house is full of their things, and you schlepp their kids all over town ... is that all there is?

DAISY: We know you spend a lot of time babysitting and chauffeuring. Don't you get tired of it? You know, it shouldn't be your job to parent your grandchildren.

BECKY: You'd think that by the time we reached our 70's we would be done parenting ...you know...have more time for ourselves. I would hope we would want a little more fun in life than being constantly on call for our grandkids who are growing up fast.

DAISY: Don't you just *love* being a chauffeur!

JUDITH: Actually, it feels good to be needed.

BECKY: I'm glad my grandson doesn't need me to drive him here and there. [Beat.] Oh, by the way, I have some exciting news.

DAISY: Did you go out with that guy your Rabbi wanted you to meet?

BECKY: No, I just found out that my Jacob and his partner are adopting a little baby girl. I'm going to be a grandmother, again.

JUDITH: That is exciting news.

DAISY: Congratulations.

BECKY: Good news, yes. But it may be a mixed blessing, because their little girl is bi-racial, and my son's partner is white, so I'm not sure I'm ready to explain why she looks so different from the rest of our family.

Act 2 - Scene 5

JUDITH: A little confusing, but nothing unusual in today's world. So, why is it a mixed blessing?

BECKY: Well, since she's a girl, we won't have to have a bris.

JUDITH: I went to a bris once and I found it fascinating.

DAISY: Can you imagine a ceremony just to watch a baby have his foreskin cut on his penis. Ouch!

BECKY: Don't get too negative, Daisy ... They soak a piece of cotton in wine and put it in the baby's mouth and basically, the baby boy is half-sedated when the actual cutting is done. Nevertheless, I'm glad she's a girl.

DAISY: Well, congratulations Becky. You know, a new grandchild usually means more work for us.

JUDITH: I would feel terrible if they didn't need me.

BECKY: Maybe in your mind grandparents are parents too, but some of us 70-year-olds wonder, "When does it end?" ... unless you're my Hershel. He stopped being a parent when Jacob came out of the closet.

JUDITH: What closet?

BECKY: Now Judith, you know what closet I'm talking about. I think he thought having a gay son was an insult to his manhood.

DAISY: Don't you think disowning your own son is a bit drastic?

JUDITH: Shouldn't Hershel have seen the clues that Jake was gay?

DAISY: Becky, tell Judith about the time Jake wanted a cowboy gun and holster set.

BECKY: Hershel was so pleased that Jacob wanted a manly toy.

DAISY: Little did he know that what drew young Jake to the set was the sparkly jewels on the holster! [Beat.]

BECKY: So, Hershel refused to see the signs for years, until Jake's senior year when he asked Joseph to be his prom date.

JUDITH: You knew Jacob was gay, but Hershel didn't. Wasn't that hard on you?

BECKY: Yes, it was difficult for me, but it was even more difficult for Jacob as he was growing up.

Act 2 - Scene 5

DAISY: Did Rivka know?

BECKY: Yes, she knew about her brother. It was always our little secret. We never stopped loving him, but once Hershel knew, our home became a battleground on this subject. I kept trying to get Hershel to accept his son the way he was and that was never going to happen. ...

DAISY: Couldn't you change his thinking?

BECKY: Once I realized that Hershel's mind was set in stone and could never be changed, I stopped arguing with him about Jacob. It was easier to just agree with him and his stupid ego.

DAISY: Why is it our job to always protect a man's ego?

JUDITH: As parents we're always protecting our children's egos.

DAISY: And then when they grow up, our children think any imperfection in their character is the fault of our parenting. [Beat.]

BECKY: Talk about unfair!

JUDITH: Even so, I love being a parent and a grandparent. It's who I am.

BECKY: Me, too! I never stopped being Jacob's mother. Once the secret was out, the hardest part was deceiving Hershel when I decided to stay in touch with Jacob.

JUDITH: Stay in touch?

BECKY: Hershel kicked Jacob out of our house, deleted him from the Will, and declared him dead when he found out his son was gay.

JUDITH: DEAD? Isn't that a bit drastic?

BECKY: That's the way it was in his mind. My husband was a typical old-fashioned, bull-headed Hungarian. He made up his mind that Jacob was dead and he was never going to budge, no matter what I said.

JUDITH: So, you came to realize that you were never going to change Hershel's mind.

BECKY: That's right. Hershel and I had separate checking accounts, so I was able to pay for Jacob's college without Hershel knowing, and I secretly kept in touch with my son.

JUDITH: Did I know you, then? Why does this sound so new? Why can't I remember this?

BECKY: That was a long time ago, and we haven't talked about it for years.

Act 2 - Scene 5

DAISY: I remember when we went to New York to see *Jersey Boys*. You suggested we take Heather so you could leave us to do our touristy things while you spent the weekend with Jacob.

BECKY: Oh, how well I remember that weekend. Jacob was so anxious to have me meet Mason, the love of his life. I was so happy for them and for me to be there for him that I almost forgot about how I had to deceive Hershel to get there. I can't tell you how many times I wanted to share those moments with my husband. ... I think he might have even liked Mason.

DAISY: Yes, it really was the perfect weekend, wasn't it? I'm glad you stuck around for *Jersey Boys* before you turned over your hotel room to Heather and me. We had a ball. We bonded and enjoyed the kinds of things that only can be seen in the Big Apple.

JUDITH: Oh, yes. Now, I remember! I recall you two humming all the familiar tunes from *Jersey Boys* when you got back from your New York get-away. [The girls start singing a familiar tune from the play. Listen to Big Girls Don't Cry by Frankie Valli on YouTube to get the right tune.]

DAISY: Yes, and I remember Heather's surprise when we knew the words to all the songs in the play.

Widows At The Club

JUDITH: How can we recall the lyrics to songs back then, when we can't remember where we put our car keys, today?

BECKY: Good question, Judith.

JUDITH: Did it ever occur to you that you were lying to Hershel? You not only were lying when you let him think you agreed to disown your son, you also lied many times over the years about your visits to New York. I remember the time when the three of us flew in for a long weekend just to see *Cats*. That was the first time I met Jacob's partner. What a great time they showed us. I can certainly understand why you secretly kept in touch with Jacob.

BECKY: Yes, you girls were always there for me and we did a great job of covering up my relationship with Jacob from Hershel.

JUDITH: [Judith sings...] *That's What Friends Are For.*

BECKY: Very nice. Yes, you and Daisy have always been there when I needed you, and now I need you both to come along with me on this trip. It's our time. Let's get on with the multiple-choice questions.

DAISY: Multiple-choice! What is this... elementary school?

BECKY: For instance, how would you answer this question ... "Are you romantic?"

Act 2 - Scene 5

[Becky and Judith look at Daisy and wait for her answer.]

DAISY: [Daisy pauses, and then blurts out.] How would I know?

BECKY: Daisy, they give you four boxes to check: "Very romantic, somewhat romantic, unsure, or not at all romantic." Pick one.

DAISY: Just to move on, I'll say, "Somewhat romantic," whatever that means. Now how would you girls answer that question?

JUDITH: Without Archie, I'd have to say I'm unsure.

BECKY: To attract a man, wouldn't we have to check, "Very romantic?"

DAISY: I thought you said we should be honest.

BECKY: Well, shouldn't we consider what we want the outcome to be?

JUDITH: You mean, getting a replacement for Archie?

BECKY: We already got the picture. You can never replace Archie, but...wouldn't it be nice to spend a quiet evening with a man that you might find interesting? Maybe someone who plays bridge.

JUDITH: There is a man in my bridge club whose wife recently passed away.

BECKY: Or Daisy might want Clark Gable with angel wings and a halo.

DAISY: Not bad, Becky! I'll drink to that! I think I'll just rush home and get that application out and say…. I want a man who looks like Clark Gable.

End of Scene 5 – Act II

Act 2 - Scene 6

Third Week of January at the Club

[Becky and Daisy enter.]

DAISY: Well, it looks like our Judith is late again. Wonder what her excuse is this week.

BECKY: I can't wait to go over some of the things we were talking about on our applications last week. I thought this was going to be easy, but....

JUDITH: [Enters.] Hi, girls! How's this for keeping my New Year's resolution?

DAISY: So ... what's your excuse for being so *early* this week?

[Becky raises her hand and circles her wrist to indicate that their drinks can be delivered.]

JUDITH: Well, I went to the doctor for my yearly check up on Monday and they sent me across the hall for my labs. You know, I was thinking of that question – "Are you Romantic?"

And ... I didn't even feel the needle going in when she was drawing blood.

BECKY: So, you were thinking about "Are you romantic?"

JUDITH: I guess that's why I didn't feel the needle.

BECKY: Aaand?

JUDITH: This afternoon I got a call from my doctor's office to read me the results of my labs and the nurse gave me a lot of numbers that didn't mean much to me, but in the end, she said everything was normal.

DAISY: Imagine that! Someone said you were normal. There's no one on this planet who's more normal than you!

JUDITH: While I was waiting to see the doctor, I picked up a magazine that had a really interesting article. It said that seniors who are sexually active are more likely to be healthy than those who are not.

BECKY: Wow! If that's the case, then I want to go to bed every night and pray for my health!

JUDITH: Eww! Becky that's gross!

BECKY: And I'm going to keep praying until I find a man!

Act 2 - Scene 6

JUDITH: Well, I guess I'll just stay celibate and unhealthy for the rest of my life.

DAISY: Mr. Schmuck certainly didn't do much for my health!

BECKY: [Hesitating] I wasn't going to say anything, but I've been going it alone with my vibrator for years. Does that mean I'm the healthy one here?

JUDITH: Eww! Becky, TMI... Shhh. Shhh.

DAISY: What's TMI?

JUDITH: Too Much Information. My grandkids are always saying that to me in their text messages ... You know, using acronyms like LOL.

BECKY and DAISY: Laughing Out Loud!

BECKY: A while back, I remember an e-mail titled something like *Acronyms for Seniors*. Of course, it was one of those joke e-mails, but some of them were really funny.

JUDITH: I got that same e-mail, too. I remember BFF. I asked my daughter what BFF stood for and she said, "Best Friends Forever." For us 70-year-olds **BFF** could stand for "Best Friend's Funeral."

BECKY: ROFL means "Rolling on the Floor Laughing" but that e-mail said ROFL ... ACGU. ... "Rolling on the Floor Laughing **And** Can't Get Up."

DAISY: You know, ever since these Smart phones came into existence nobody talks on the phone. They just text to each other using lots of initials. Between my new smart phone and new computer, I think I'm going crazy!

JUDITH: I mostly use my computer to send and receive e-mails, and I got an e-mail the other day from a friend. She wrote IMHO. I thought she was talking about her HMO. So, I asked her what she meant by IMHO. I laughed when she told me it meant "In My Humble Opinion." This is so confusing.

DAISY So far, I spend most of my time playing solitaire on my new laptop. If I wanted to text, I would probably send you a note saying HGBM – "Had Good Bowel Movement."

BECKY: Yeah, and I could write JK.

JUDITH: What is JK?

BECKY: "Just Kvetching."

JUDITH: Only a Jewish princess like you would understand that one.

Act 2 - Scene 6

[Prop person delivers drinks.]

DAISY: Becky, did you say you've had a relationship with your vibrator for years?

BECKY: Hey, it's time we all got into the 21st century. A few years ago, I got up at about three o'clock in the morning to pee and couldn't fall back to sleep so ... I started flicking through the channels on the TV. I became glued to the screen while two women were showing and discussing an array of vibrators and other sex toys. And, just like the QVC channel they made it easy to purchase a vibrator right there on the TV.

JUDITH: Oh, my God! Shhh!

BECKY: I don't remember the channel, but I did see it a few more times on other nights when I took my pee-pee break. They even showed sex toys for men. I didn't know such things existed! ... And for sure I never thought I'd live to see the day when these things were advertised on TV.

JUDITH: This is really TMI. Too Much Information for me.

DAISY: What a time we're living in! We've got candidates for President and professional athletes talking about their erections and vibrators being advertised on TV!

JUDITH: My daughter told me her youngest son asked her what an erection was. After a long pause, she had an inspiration and finally told her son: ..." Elections are for voters."

DAISY: Did he fall for that cheesy answer?

JUDITH: Yup! He seemed happy just to get an answer and went back to playing with his motorized erector set.

BECKY: So, let's get back to answering the question about being romantic. Who would have thought that dating at our age could be so complicated? After all, you know we've done this before.

DAISY: Done what?

BECKY: Dating!

JUDITH: But we were so much younger then!

DAISY: All I know is that there are a lot of DOM's out there!

JUDITH: DOM's?

DAISY: Dirty Old Men!

JUDITH: Well, Archie was never a Dirty Old Man!

Act 2 - Scene 6

DAISY: Hey, my phone is vibrating. ... So, I really need to take this call.

JUDITH: Vibrating? [Judith and Becky look knowingly at each other.]

DAISY: Hello? Oh, Hi Heather. ... Yes, I'm at the club having dinner with Judith and Becky, but I can talk. [Daisy gestures that she needs to go out to finish her call.] I'll be right back. [Daisy takes her "flip phone" and leaves through the door.]

BECKY: A phone call at this time of night can't be good.

JUDITH: It's not that late.

BECKY: [The girls look at their forms.] I had to chuckle when I got to the question: What religion do you practice? Does that mean they are practicing so they can get better at religion?

JUDITH: Or are they practicing because they are rusty?

BECKY: Is it a game and they need to practice more often to get better at the game?

JUDITH: They should have asked: What *is* your religion?

BECKY: Yeah. That's a much better way to put it. [Pause while looking at her form.] You know Judith, I think *most* of these websites are very concerned about making good matches for their clients. In fact, on *Rent-a-Yenta*, I read a few testimonials of some very successful matches.

JUDITH: Really? [Hesitantly] I guess if I thought *Play-It-Again-Sam* could give me another Archie, I just might be interested.

BECKY: Hershel was an excellent companion when we went to a play, the Symphony, or visited the Art Museum. I'd be happy just to meet a nice man who could enjoy these things with me.

JUDITH: Yes, that would be nice.

[Daisy enters.]

BECKY: So, what did Heather have to say?

DAISY: Wonderful! It's official. My daughter has finally filed for divorce!

BECKY and JUDITH: Ooh!

DAISY: And ... you want to know if I'm romantic? My son-in-law is useless. My son is useless. Mr. Schmuck was useless. Every man I know is worthless! Don't ask me if I'm romantic!

JUDITH: Oh, Daisy.

Act 2 - Scene 6

BECKY: [Reaching out to Daisy.] I'm confused. Good news; bad news. Are you happy or upset?

DAISY: Both! I'm glad Heather has finally made the big decision to dump that husband of hers. After just hearing this, though, I'm agitated by all these questions ... "Are you romantic?" [Daisy shakes her head.] I just want to eat and go home.

End of Scene 6 – Act II

Act 2 - Scene 7

Fourth Week of January at the Club

[Becky & Daisy enter.]

BECKY: The roads were really slippery tonight. Did you hit any icy patches on your way?

DAISY: No. The roads were plowed pretty good.

BECKY: Judith called to tell me she thought she'd be late because she had to take her granddaughter to basketball practice, and she wasn't sure she could even get here because of the roads. We'll give her a few minutes to call if she's not coming tonight.

DAISY: If she can drive to a lousy practice, she can drive here! Where are her priorities?

BECKY: Do you think she was afraid I might force her to commit to online dating during cocktails?

DAISY: Could be. Who knows what she might agree to once she's liquored up!

BECKY: I wish that's all it would take to get her on board!

DAISY: Since she doesn't allow any time for herself, I doubt she'll ever make time to date again. We know Archie was not as perfect as she says he was.

BECKY: Do you think she'll ever admit that?

DAISY: I don't know if she'll ever admit it, but I remember how she complained about his smoking. He even lied to her about quitting. I remember when she told us he used to go outside and light up behind the garage. She was furious at him.

BECKY: Yes, and she was always complaining about him spending too much time on the golf course and not enough time with the kids.

DAISY: Sir Galahad had chinks in his armor. [Beat.]

BECKY: Keeping Archie up on a pedestal is probably her excuse for not wanting to get involved with online dating. She must realize that those kids will soon grow up and they won't need her. And then what?

Act 2 - Scene 7

DAISY: She's not going to think that far ahead. She's only thinking of helping her grown children take care of their kids because they work.

BECKY: When we first married, we didn't have such big fancy houses and expensive cars, and many of us were stay-at-home-moms. Seems like today's young parents want to start where we left off. [Beat.]

DAISY: And our kids didn't have to go to private schools, either.

BECKY: Zack did just fine in the public schools.

DAISY: Would it hurt them if they didn't attend the most prestigious schools?

BECKY: Some employers won't even look at a new hire these days without that pedigree.
[Judith enters.]

JUDITH: Pedigree? Is someone getting a new dog?

DAISY: All hail, the queen has arrived!

[Becky raises her hand and circles her wrist to indicate that their drinks can be delivered.]

JUDITH: Hi, girls.

Widows At The Club

DAISY: Oh, tell us, mighty princess, what doth bringeth thee to us at this slightly late hour? Speak on, oh wise one.

JUDITH: I swear, I might forget to bring my head if it weren't attached!

BECKY: What happened?

JUDITH: Let's see. Out to the car; no car keys. Out to the car, again; no folder. Drop my granddaughter at church for practice. Then I stopped at the store and when I got out, I forgot where I parked! I'm beginning to worry about Alzheimer's!

BECKY: Don't worry. That kind of thing happens to all of us at one time or another. Those filing cabinets in our brains just get overloaded.

DAISY: Not so fast! This episode of the Twilight Zone is brought to you by Mother Dementia's little memory pills! This could be serious! We should all keep track of these moments. There's nothing scarier than Alzheimer's.

BECKY: There's no need for record-keeping. It's not that big a deal. Life is too short to be wasted worrying about something that might never happen.

DAISY: Oh, come on. You know I was just kidding.

Act 2 - Scene 7

BECKY: Judith, aren't some of your grandchildren getting close to driving age?

JUDITH: Yes, but ....

BECKY: You know that day is right around the corner when you won't be needed by them. They start to drive, they get a social life, and guess who's left with NO social life.

JUDITH: Are you looking at me? I dread the day when they won't need me.

DAISY: They probably don't need you now. Their parents need you. If it were not for your availability to take those kids everywhere, their parents wouldn't be able to indulge themselves in whatever they do.

BECKY: Don't you think it's time for your own activities? You know, going to the theater, dining out with a companion, a walk in the woods. You know, like having a date?

DAISY: I could imagine myself going on a cruise with someone other than Heather and the kids.

BECKY: Hmmm. I wouldn't mind meeting a man who would take me on a cruise.

JUDITH: If I met a man and if he wanted to take me on a cruise, I would insist on two separate cabins.

DAISY: Then, why even go?

[Prop person delivers drinks and Judith's vodka. Judith nods.]

JUDITH: I have to admit, with Archie gone, I'm not quite sure what to do with the rest of my life. I've got my grandchildren. Can't that be all I need?

BECKY: They will grow up, leave the nest, and stop needing you.

JUDITH: What a depressing thought!

DAISY: Why do we have to grandparent to earn the right to be fulfilled? Lately, I find no pleasure around my grandchildren. Heather's daughter started to teach me to use the computer, but got tired of that in a hurry. They are so deep into their own thing they hardly notice I'm in the room.

JUDITH: Yes, I'm starting to get the same feeling, these days.

BECKY: When they grow up and stop needing you where does that leave you?

DAISY: Oh, Becky, you're a sly one! I see you're leading us back to online dating!

BECKY: Never left.

Act 2 - Scene 7

JUDITH: I know that there will never be a man who can replace Archie.

BECKY: Don't think of it as replacing Archie; think of it as enhancing your life. How will you ever know unless you try?

DAISY: Let me tell you, I assumed that when my daughter was grown up with a family of her own, I would be free to enjoy travel and whatever stupid thing I wanted to do. You know "freedom!"

BECKY: I agree. When we were young, our kids needed us, and we were there for them. I thought when we got to this age, we might need help from our kids and they would be there for us.

DAISY: Wishful thinking.

BECKY: They mean well, but they're all wrapped up in their own lives with all their own problems. [Becky pauses to think.] All the more reason for us to think about ourselves more!

DAISY: I can't remember. Was dating fun?

BECKY: I think so.

DAISY: Ah ha! I caught you! Even <u>you</u> aren't completely sure this dating thing is a good idea!

Widows At The Club

BECKY: I'd feel a lot more comfortable doing this, if we were all in this together. Nothing's a sure thing. I just want to give it a try.

DAISY: Becky, we know you want to give it a try...It's the only thing on your mind for the last two months.

JUDITH: Are you saying this is not pretending anymore?

BECKY: I'm not pretending, but I need both of you to help me. Maybe Heather could join us after she gets her divorce. What a great addition she would make to our group!

DAISY: I'm glad Heather has finally decided to make her move. She's finally going to get rid of 250 pounds of ugly, lazy fat!

BECKY: Think of all the money she's going to save at the grocery store!

JUDITH: We're talking about ADDING men to our lives, but Heather is SUBTRACTING!

DAISY: Sometimes subtracting is the best way to go! Maybe I should have done that years ago!

JUDITH: What are you going to do with a houseful of grandchildren and a divorced daughter?

Act 2 - Scene 7

DAISY: Whoa, hold your horses, Calamity Jane! Don't you remember, the schmuck owned a ton of rental units around town. She has already picked out the one she will move into...just her and the kids.

BECKY: So, Heather gets a divorce and will make a stab at a whole new life for herself and you will still be alone.

DAISY: I would be alone even if the kids were around. They don't play with human beings like we did as kids. They play all those killer type games all day long.

JUDITH: I agree. If there were NO smart phones, they might actually need to have friends that they talk to in person.

BECKY: Or friends that they play with.

DAISY: You mean play like we used to do. Jump rope, hop-scotch, jacks.

JUDITH: Yes, and I remember on rainy days, we invited our friends over, and we played pick-up sticks.

BECKY: And, Tiddlywinks.

JUDITH: At our house we had an old shoebox full of crayons and we colored on lace doilies and coloring books.

BECKY: Speaking about kids moving in, my Jacob is moving back to town with his partner and my new granddaughter. I can't wait to wrap my arms around that little bugger.

DAISY: What brought this on?

BECKY: Well, you know after Hershel died and left me with the store to run, I have been a very busy lady, so...I have been talking to Jacob about coming back to town and taking over for me.

JUDITH: Hershel would turn over in his grave.

BECKY: You're probably right, but Jacob is my son and I love him, and Mason is wonderful.

DAISY: Isn't Jacob General Manager of a similar store in New York?

BECKY: Yes, and we've been talking for a long time about this possibility. He has a lot of good ideas about how to bring Hershel's store into the 21st Century.

JUDITH: Aren't you worried about your gay son, his partner, and their biracial baby being accepted in this little bedroom community?

BECKY: They won't be living in the 'Burbs, Judith. They're looking at renovating one of those big old mansions in the

Act 2 - Scene 7

near downtown area where the neighborhood is more diverse. They'll be just fine, and it will be more house than they ever dreamed of having while living in New York.

JUDITH: Let me see if I've got this right. You talk your son into taking over the family business, so you can be free to flit around the world with a new beau in your life.

BECKY: Well ...

JUDITH: Now I get it. I always thought there was an ulterior motive for dragging us into your little scheme of "meeting men."

BECKY: Maybe that is so, but ... I thought it might be nice for all of us to add a little spice to our lives. I admit that I would feel more comfortable if I had my friends in this with me.

JUDITH: Add some spice. You've got a point. I probably do need to ease up on "grandparenting" a bit.

BECKY: Now, you're being flexible!

[Becky and Judith turn to Daisy expectantly.]

DAISY: Well, with my arthritis, I probably should ease up on golf and Pickleball a bit.

BECKY and JUDITH: Aand ...

DAISY: Aand that might give me enough time for a man in my life. If there is such a thing as a good man.

BECKY: That's the spirit!

DAISY: Don't get too excited. I'm still not on the hunt for a man. I'm trying to be flexible because we all agreed to this little experiment. But, if a good man fell in my lap, I'm willing to give him a look.

BECKY: Well, maybe Heather would find this interesting enough to look for a decent guy once she rids herself of her schlemiel.

DAISY: Hey, she's not even divorced yet, and here we are, trying to marry her off. Give me a break.

BECKY: Maybe Heather will teach you how to insert your photo on this application.

JUDITH: And, maybe she will talk you into getting rid of that "flip phone."

DAISY: I have a confession to make. I've fallen off the cliff! I bought a smart phone and Heather is helping me understand my laptop and smart phone. What more can I do?

BECKY: You could stop hanging on to that flip-phone, and start using your new phone.

Act 2 - Scene 7

DAISY: You're right. I guess I'm just a slow learner.

JUDITH: Welcome to the 21st century!

BECKY: Good for you! That's a big deal! I'm sure Zack would also be glad to help you. He was excited to help me post my mug shots on my application.

JUDITH: Do you think Zack would help me post my photos, if I ever could find one without grandchildren in the picture?

BECKY: Zack taught me how to do a selfie on my phone. Maybe you could do that.

DAISY: Hey, you have six grandchildren. Surely one of them would teach you to do this.

JUDITH: I'm not telling anyone in my family about our little experiment.

DAISY: Really? I told Heather and she's been really supportive.

BECKY: Yes, I'm pretty sure my Zack would do that for any of us. We can all help each other.

JUDITH: Remember, we just had the funeral for my sister-in-law. And I must admit, that did get me thinking about how fragile life is, and how we shouldn't waste what little time we have left. So, I'm starting to understand why you want us to do this.

BECKY: You're right Judith. It's like this. This is our life, [Becky holds her hands at least 4 feet apart.] and this is how much time we have left. [Becky brings her hands together about six inches apart.]

DAISY: So, you're telling us we should make the most of what's left. [Daisy holds her hands six inches apart.]

JUDITH: Yes Daisy…. Becky is making a good argument.

BECKY: So … it's official. Seems like we are all ready to do this. We're all going to do this for real! [To Daisy.] Are you in?

DAISY: As long as we all do this together.

BECKY: That's two of us for sure. Judith?

JUDITH: Oh, alright.

[Becky stands with her drink glass in hand…Daisy rises followed timidly by Judith.]

BECKY: Bring it on! Let the fun and games begin!

Act 2 - Scene 7

ALL THREE: [All three raise their glasses.] ***BRING IT ON!*** [Beat.] [Beat.]

DAISY: [Daisy sits back down and slaps her forehead.] Heaven help us!

Curtain down...The End

Afterword

Leading up to writing **"Widows at the Club"** their eyes met, then their hearts met, and soon their creative minds met. They wrote their play.

Shortly after her book was published a new Pickleball player began showing up in Bea's pickleball group. His name was Dave. Their first gab session after Pickleball one day led to a three-hour marathon at a nearby coffee shop where they learned how much they had in common. Both had lost their spouses about three years prior to this meeting.

Widows At The Club

There was no stopping them after that first outing away from the Pickleball crowd. Bea and Dave soon became a "thing". It didn't take them long to realize they wanted to be together permanently so they both sold their homes and bought and furnished a beautiful Condo in New Albany, Oh.

Due to the Covid 19 pandemic, the dating scene was pretty much confined to just the two of them and that was when they decided to write a play together. They began by adapting a lot of the discussions in the play from different aspects of Bea's book **"Bring It On...We're In Our 70's"** and that was the beginning of their two act play titled **"Widows At The Club"**.

Subsequently, this awesome twosome was accepted in the New Writers Initiative at Curtain Players and along with 5 other playwriters, they were able to polish and complete **"Widows at the Club"**. In other words, they got their play stage ready.

On January 8, 2022, Curtain Players turned the theater over to Bea and Dave for a staged reading of their two-act play. The three actors and the director brought **"Widows At The Club"** to life in front of a live audience ....a dream come true for Bea and Dave. The **"talk back"** live from the audience after the performance gave credence to the success of their endeavors.

Afterword

Sad to say, shortly after their debut with the staged reading Dave took ill. "It wasn't supposed to happen," said Bea. "The pandemic was over, and we were ready to follow up on a few venues for our play and travel around the country during this time. But unfortunately, Dave's health issues were taking center stage and everything else was put on the back burner." With great sorrow and sadness Dave passed away in September of 2022.

Bea says, "Feel free to contact her if you know anyone who might be interested in presenting **Widows At The Club** at any local community theater. If would work well as a full production or as a "Staged reading" in a black box theater with a **talk back** afterwards.

Bea Gardner   772-539-1877   www.beagardner.com

www.ingramcontent.com/pod-product-compliance
Lightning Source LLC
Chambersburg PA
CBHW020947090426
42736CB00010B/1299